W9-BZT-294

Finding Shortest and Longest

By Amy Rauen

Reading consultant: Susan Nations, M.Ed.,
author/literacy coach/consultant in literacy development

Math consultant: Rhea Stewart, M.A., mathematics content specialist

WEEKLY READER®
PUBLISHING

Please visit our web site at www.garethstevens.com
For a free color catalog describing our list of high-quality books,
call 1-800-542-2595 (USA) or 1-800-387-3178 (Canada). Our fax: 1-877-542-2596

Library of Congress Cataloging-in-Publication Data

Rauen, Amy.
    Finding shortest and longest / Amy Rauen.
        p. cm. — (Getting started with math)
    ISBN-13: 978-0-8368-8982-6 (lib. bdg.)
    ISBN-10: 0-8368-8982-7 (lib. bdg.)
    ISBN-13: 978-0-8368-8987-1 (softcover)
    ISBN-10: 0-8368-8987-8 (softcover)
    1. Length measurement—Juvenile literature. 2. Depth perception—Juvenile
literature. I. Title.
    QC102.R37   2008
    516'.15—dc22   2007026317

This edition first published in 2008 by
Weekly Reader® Books
An Imprint of Gareth Stevens Publishing
1 Reader's Digest Road
Pleasantville, NY 10570-7000 USA

Senior Editor: Brian Fitzgerald
Creative Director: Lisa Donovan
Graphic Designer: Alexandria Davis

Photo credits: cover, title page, pp. 6, 7, 8, 9, 10, 11, 12, 13 Russell Pickering;
p. 4 © Ariel Skelley/Corbis; p. 5 Abode/Beateworks/Corbis; p. 15 Weekly Reader Archives.

Printed in the United States of America

1 2 3 4 5 6 7 8 9 10 09 08 07

Note to Educators and Parents

Reading is such an exciting adventure for young children! They are beginning to match the spoken word to print and learn directionality and print conventions, among other skills. Books that are appropriate for emergent readers incorporate these conventions while also informing and entertaining them.

The books in the *Getting Started With Math* series are designed to support young readers in the earliest stages of literacy. Readers will love looking at the full-color photographs and illustrations as they develop skills in early math concepts. This integration allows young children to maximize their learning as they see how thoughts and ideas connect across content areas.

In addition to serving as wonderful picture books in schools, libraries, and homes, the *Getting Started With Math* books are specifically intended to be read within guided small reading groups. The small group setting enables the teacher or other adult to provide scaffolding that will boost the reader's effort. Children and adults alike will find these books supportive, engaging, and fun!

Susan Nations, M.Ed.
author/literacy coach/consultant in literacy development

This is our home.
My family lives here.

We have things of
many lengths.

The shortest shoe is pink.

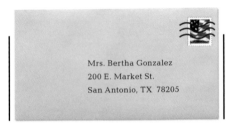

The longest letter is blue.
It is for my dad.

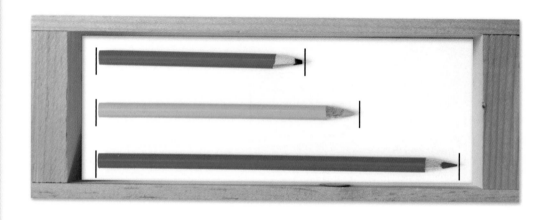

The shortest pencil is green.
It is in a box.

The longest spoon is wooden.
My mom stirs things with it.

The shortest picture is of a flower.

The red car is longest.
Red is my favorite color.

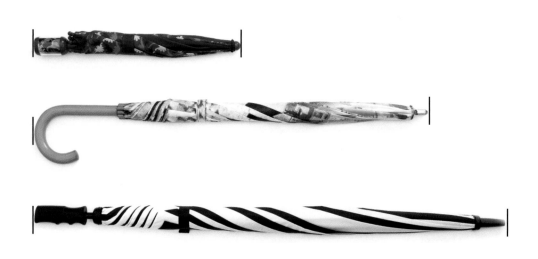

The shortest umbrella is blue.

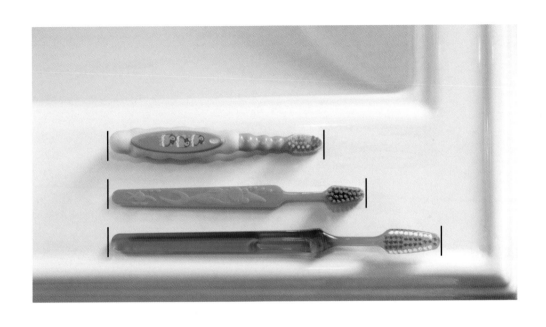

My toothbrush is on top.
It is the shortest!

Glossary

letter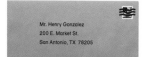

shortest

longest

spoon

pencil

toothbrush

picture

toy

shoe

umbrella

Show What You Know

1. Which of the three leaves is longest?

2. Which is shortest: the spoon, the fork, or the knife?

To Find Out More

The Best Bug Parade. Mathstart (series).
Stuart J. Murphy (HarperCollins Children's Books)

Tall and Short. Sizes (series).
Diane Nieker (Heinemann Read and Learn)

About the Author

Amy Rauen is the author of more than a dozen math books for children. She also designs and writes educational software. Amy lives in San Diego, California, with her husband and their two cats.